EXPLORING OUR SENSES

Smelling

For a free color catalog describing Gareth Stevens' list of high-quality books, call 1-800-542-2595 (USA) or 1-800-461-9120 (Canada). Gareth Stevens' Fax: (414) 225-0377.

Library of Congress Cataloging-in-Publication Data

Pluckrose, Henry Arthur.
  Smelling/by Henry Pluckrose; photographs by Chris Fairclough.
    p. cm. -- (Exploring our senses)
  Includes bibliographical references and index.
  Summary: Text and photographs present smells found in a bakery,
shoe store, garden, and around the house.
    ISBN 0-8368-1289-1
    1. Smell--Juvenile literature. [1. Smell. 2. Senses and sensation.]
  I. Fairclough, Chris, ill. II. Title. III. Series.
  QP458.P55   1995
  612.8'6--dc20   94-23775

13283
9/00

North American edition first published in 1995 by
Gareth Stevens Publishing
1555 North RiverCenter Drive, Suite 201
Milwaukee, Wisconsin 53212, USA

Additional photographs: Eye Ubiquitous 24; Photos Horticultural 15; ZEFA 16, 24.

Printed in the United States of America

1 2 3 4 5 6 7 8 9 99 98 97 96 95

Smelling

By Henry Pluckrose
Photographs by Chris Fairclough

Gareth Stevens Publishing
MILWAUKEE

The world is
full of things
to smell —
some pleasant . . .

and some terrible.

Think of all
these different
smells —
ripe fruit . . .

6

fresh bread . . .

strong cheese . . .

8

hot pizza . . .

9

shampoos, bath oils, and perfumes . . .

leather and
polish . . .

11

and gasoline at
the filling station.

12

In a garden,
you might smell
the sweet scent
of flowers . . .

the earthiness
of dead leaves
or wet soil . . .

or the heavy scent
of cut grass.

15

In cities,
we live with
the strong fumes
of cars and trucks . . .

the stench
of hot tar . . .

and the reek of smoke
from factories.

Not all smells
are pleasant.
Have you smelled
the odors of wastes
pouring into the sea?

Have you smelled a field being sprayed . . .

or the sour odor
of dirty water?

What things do you
most like to smell —
the saltiness of the sea . . .

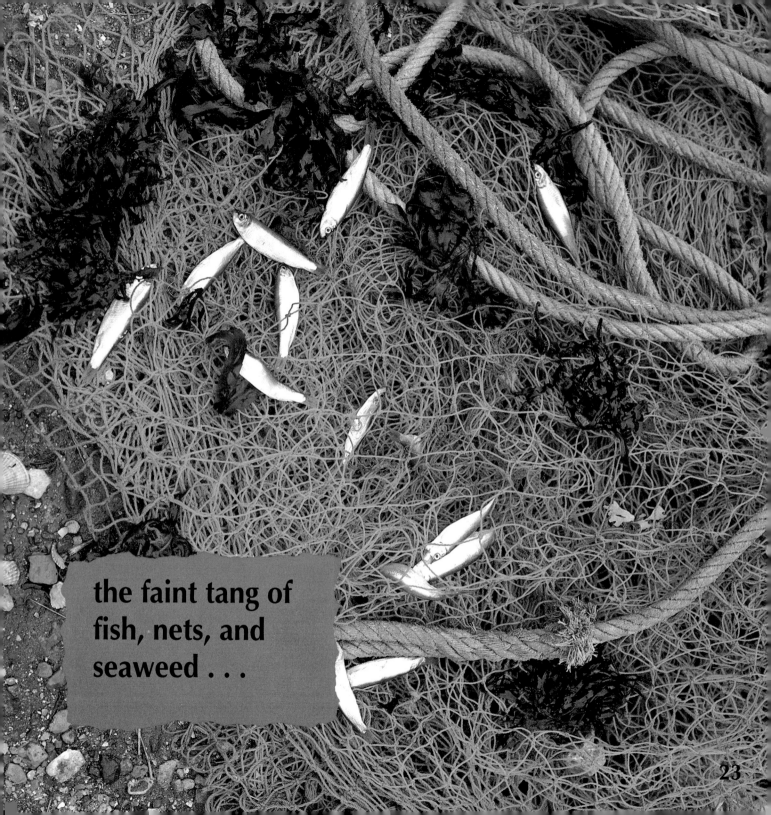

the faint tang of fish, nets, and seaweed . . .

23

the warmth
of horses . . .

newly cut wood . . .

the fresh smell
of shampoo . . .

26

or ironed
clothes?

Which food smell tempts you more — steaming apple pie . . .

or a baked potato with melting butter?

Which do
you think
smells nicer —
flowers . . .

30

or fruity soaps?
What is your
favorite smell?

More Books to Read

Professor I.Q. Explores the Senses. Seymour Simon (Bell)
Smelling. Kathie B. Smith (Troll)
Teach Me About Smelling. Joy Wilt (Childrens Press)

Videotapes

You and Your Five Senses. (Disney)
You — And Your Sense of Smell and Taste. (Disney)

Activities for Learning and Fun

1. Potpourri Make some sweet-smelling potpourri with dried herbs, flowers, and spices. Begin by drying the petals from roses or other fragrant flowers on a cookie sheet placed in a warm, dry location. After the petals have dried, add other sweet-smelling ingredients, such as orange peels, cinnamon, cloves, or lavender. Shake all the ingredients in a bag. Place the potpourri in a shallow bowl to keep all the noses in your house happy!

2. Show and Smell Use scratch-and-sniff stickers to help illustrate a story you have written. Purchase a variety of stickers at a card or novelty store. Think about how the stickers can be used as part of your story. Then use the stickers as part of the illustration for each page. Can scratching and sniffing the stickers be part of the action of your story?

Index